D1012135

Cook It in a Cup!

Quick Meals and Treats
Kids Can Cook in Silicone Cups

By Julia Myall

Photographs by Greg Lowe

chronicle books · san francisco

For my kids, who inspired me to create yummy recipes,
and who are always willing to educate their palates!
— J. M.

Text © 2008 by Julia Myall.
Photos © 2008 by Greg Lowe.
All rights reserved.

Oreo is a registered trademark of Kraft Foods Holding, Inc.

Book design by Mariana Oldenburg.
Typeset in Triplex and Zemke Hand.
Manufactured in China.

Library of Congress Cataloging-in-Publication Data
Myall, Julia.
Cook it in a cup! : quick meals and treats kids can cook in
silicone cups / by Julia Myall ; photographs by Greg Lowe.
   p. cm.
 ISBN 978-0-8118-5956-1
 1. Quick and easy cookery. I. Title.
 TX833.5.M92 2008
 641.5'55—dc22
 2007010482

10 9 8 7 6 5 4 3

Chronicle Books LLC
680 Second Street, San Francisco, California 94107

www.chroniclekids.com

Table of Contents

Sweet Treats

Compliments to the Chef!

Not Just for Cupcakes!

They're fun . . . they're flexible . . . and they come in great colors. But what can you do with them? Lots! You can make pasta, bake lemon bars, scramble an egg, and much more. The recipes in this book are only the *beginning* of what you can do.

Sure, they may *look* like cupcake holders, but really silicone cups have endless possibilities. You can bake, roast, microwave, and freeze with them. Plus, silicone is nonstick, so your finished recipes slide out easily and cleanup is quick (no scrubbing!).

The cups are bendable and flexible— even turn-inside-out-able! That means you can peel back their sides to help get the food out, and you can turn them inside out to wash them. The cups are also easy to handle after cooking, because they're cool to the touch within a few minutes of leaving the oven.

The recipes in this book are for meals, side dishes, snacks, and sweets. None of them will take you too long to make, but all of them are delicious! Many of the recipes were designed so you can make as little or as much as you want. You can whip up a quick snack for yourself; you can cook for a group of friends after school, or you can make the main course, side dish, or dessert for a family dinner. Hey, you can even make the whole dinner with your silicone cups!

You'll find plenty of good-for-you (but still good!) recipes in this book. You'll discover new ways to cook vegetables with great flavors, and you'll get acquainted with new side dishes. You'll also find a super-simple method for making an egg sandwich—a great protein snack—on page 10. See what you think!

Fast, fun, good for you, and easy—these things make cooking exciting for chefs. So, pick out a recipe, grab your cups and your ingredients, and let's get cooking!

Using Your Cups

You are now the proud owner of six colorful, bendable, wonderful silicone cups. Here are a few tips to keep in mind when you use them.

Wash 'em first
Wash and dry your cups before using them the first time.

Beware of hot stuff
Always use a hot pad or an oven mitt when handling cups that are fresh from the oven. Soon after cooking, the edges of the cup may be cool, but the part with the food in it will still be hot. So be careful! And don't forget about steam. All food releases steam when cooked, so watch out for hot steam when you're turning food out of your cups.

Stuck in the cup?
If something doesn't slide right out of a cup, give it more time to cool. Then try gently squeezing the base, using an oven mitt if the cup is still too warm to touch. Squeeze the base a few times in different spots, and then try to release the food again. If that doesn't help, slide a spoon or a butter knife between the edge of the cup and the food to help ease it out.

Clean up in a snap!

Cleaning your cups is easy. You can give them a quick wash with a soapy sponge in the sink, or you can put them in the top rack of the dishwasher.

Kitchen Safety

You'll see this symbol ⚠ whenever a recipe step involves cutting with a sharp knife, using a kitchen appliance, or handling hot things. That's when you should be *especially* careful. Ask for adult help whenever the step requires it, or whenever you're doing something that's totally new to you.

Also, when an ingredient list calls for a pre-chopped item, ask an adult for help, especially if the item is tough to cut or if you're just not used to chopping. No matter what, an adult should be around whenever you're cooking, so you can get help anytime you need it.

Breakfast in a Cup

Easy Eggs

Ingredients for each cup:

1 egg

Serving Suggestions:
- Toast, bagel, or English muffin
- Cheese
- Ham or Turkey

These eggs are great protein snacks, and they come out the perfect shape for putting on a bagel, an English muffin, or a piece of toast. Add a slice of ham, turkey, or cheese for a delicious breakfast sandwich!

I. Crack the egg into a measuring cup and stir with a fork until it's well blended. Pour the egg into a baking cup.

2. Microwave the egg on high for 30 seconds.

3. Let the egg cool for about 2 minutes, then turn it out of the cup to serve.

Tomato, **Bell Pepper, and Olive Frittata**

> *A frittata is an Italian version of an omelet. Frittatas can have all sorts of ingredients mixed into them, so feel free to use only your favorites!*

Ingredients for 6 frittatas:

4 eggs
$1/4$ cup milk
Pinch of salt
Pinch of pepper
$1/2$ cup shredded Monterey Jack cheese
$1/2$ tomato, chopped
$1/2$ bell pepper, seeded and chopped
2 tablespoons chopped black olives

1. Preheat the oven to 350°F.

2. Crack the eggs into a large measuring cup. Add the milk, salt, and pepper and stir with a fork until blended. Then add the cheese and stir again.

3. Combine the tomato, bell pepper, and olives in a small bowl and mix well. Then fill each cup halfway with the vegetables.

4. Pour the egg mixture on top of the vegetables, filling the cups three-fourths full.

5. Place the cups on a baking sheet and bake for 10 minutes, or until no liquid is visible in the center. Let cool for 2 minutes, then carefully turn the frittatas out of the cups to serve. ⚠

Banana–Chocolate Chip Muffins

Ingredients for 12 muffins:

1¹/₂ cups all-purpose flour
1 teaspoon baking soda
¹/₂ teaspoon ground nutmeg
¹/₂ teaspoon ground cinnamon
Pinch of salt
¹/₂ cup (1 stick) butter, softened
1 cup sugar
1 cup mashed ripe banana (2 bananas)
1 egg
1 teaspoon vanilla extract
1 cup semisweet chocolate chips

These sweet, moist muffins are delicious for breakfast, especially when served warm with butter. And with your silicone cups, there's no need for paper liners!

1. Preheat the oven to 350°F.

2. Combine the flour, baking soda, nutmeg, cinnamon, and salt in a medium bowl and stir to mix. Set aside.

3. Combine the butter and sugar in a medium bowl. Mix with a fork until creamy and smooth.

4. Add the banana, egg, and vanilla and mix until combined.

5. Slowly add the flour mixture to the butter mixture and stir with a fork until well combined. Stir in the chocolate chips.

6. Spoon half of the batter into the 6 cups, filling the cups two-thirds full.

7. Place the cups on a baking sheet and bake for 20 minutes, or until a butter knife or a toothpick inserted into the center of a muffin comes out clean. ⚠️

8. Let the muffins cool for 5 minutes, and then peel away the cups. Refill the cups to make 6 more muffins the same way. ⚠️

Try it this way!

• Not a big chocolate fan? Use a cup of chopped nuts instead. Or try a cup of raisins.

• For pumpkin-chocolate muffins, use a cup of canned pumpkin purée in place of the banana.

Crumb Cakes

Ingredients for 12 cakes:

Cakes

- 2 cups all-purpose flour
- 1 teaspoon salt
- 1 tablespoon baking powder
- ½ cup (1 stick) butter, softened
- 1½ cups granulated sugar
- 2 eggs
- ¾ cup milk
- 1 container (8 ounces) vanilla yogurt

(Ingredients continued on next page.)

These crumb cakes are buttery and rich, and the crown of toasty crumbs adds a nice cinnamon crunch. Treat someone to breakfast in bed with them!

To Make the Cakes

1. Combine the flour, salt, and baking powder in a medium bowl and mix well. Set aside.

2. Combine the butter and sugar in a medium bowl and mix with a fork until creamy.

3. Add the eggs, milk, and yogurt and mix with a fork until smooth.

4. Slowly add the flour mixture to the butter mixture and stir with a fork until combined.

5. Arrange the cups on a baking sheet and spoon half of the batter into the 6 cups, filling them to the top.

To Make the Crumb Topping and Bake the Cakes

1. Preheat the oven to 350°F.

2. Combine the brown sugar, granulated sugar, flour, cinnamon, and butter in a medium bowl. Mix with a fork until you have pea-size crumbs.

3. Using half of the topping, sprinkle an equal amount on each filled cup.

4. Bake the cakes for 20 minutes, or until a toothpick or butter knife inserted into the cakes comes out clean. ⚠

5. Let cool for 10 minutes, then turn the cakes out of the cups. Refill the cups to make 6 more cakes the same way. ⚠

Ingredients continued:

Crumb Topping
 ½ cup light brown sugar, lightly packed
 ½ cup granulated sugar
 6 tablespoons all-purpose flour
 1 tablespoon ground cinnamon
 ½ cup (1 stick) butter, softened

Ham and Cheese Popovers

Ingredients for 6 popovers:

1 package (10.1 ounces)
refrigerated croissant or crescent-
roll dough (for 6 croissants)
1 cup chopped ham
1 cup shredded Cheddar cheese

Thanks to ready-made croissant dough, you can whip up these tasty popovers really fast! For a sweet version, substitute cinnamon and sugar—a sprinkle of each—for the ham and cheese.

1. Preheat the oven to 425°F.

2. Unroll the dough and separate the 6 triangles.

3. Sprinkle an equal amount of the ham and cheese on the center of each triangle. Roll up each triangle as shown above.

4. The rolls will have some extra dough on the ends. Trim this off (about half an inch on each end).

5. Place each roll in a cup. Then place the cups on a baking sheet and bake for 10 minutes, or until puffed and golden brown. Let cool for 2 minutes, then turn the rolls out of the cups to serve. ⚠

Mini Main Courses

Little Lasagnas

Ingredients for 6 lasagnas:

1½ cups dried penne pasta
1½ cups tomato sauce
½ cup ricotta cheese
3 tablespoons shredded mozzarella cheese
1½ teaspoons grated Parmesan cheese
1½ teaspoons minced fresh basil
1 small clove garlic, minced
Pinch of salt
Pinch of pepper
Extra Parmesan cheese for sprinkling

It takes a long time to make a big lasagna, but these little ones are ready in a flash! Plus, you can use different pastas or fillings to customize your mini lasagnas, so each one can be different.

1. Preheat the oven to 350°F.

2. Put ¼ cup of the penne pasta and ¼ cup of the tomato sauce in each cup. Mix well to coat pasta with sauce.

3. Combine the three cheeses with the basil, garlic, salt, and pepper in a medium bowl. Mix with a fork.

4. Top each cup with 2 tablespoons of the cheese mixture.

5. Sprinkle an extra pinch of Parmesan cheese on top of each cup.

6. Place the cups on a baking sheet, cover with aluminum foil, and bake for about 20 minutes, or until the sauce is bubbling. Serve in or out of the cups. To serve outside of the cups, use a spoon to scoop out the lasagnas. ⚠

Try it this way!

• You can make this recipe with other kinds of pasta. If you like a softer texture, try angel hair pasta. Break the pasta into small pieces so it'll fit in the cups.

• You can also add chopped spinach for a bit of green, or chopped, cooked chicken sausage. Add any or all of these items to the cheese mixture in step 3. About 2 tablespoons of each should do it.

Mini **Meat** Loaves

Ingredients for 12 meat loaves:

$1/2$ red onion, chopped

1 clove garlic

1 carrot, peeled and chopped

$1/2$ cup grated Parmesan cheese

1 pound ground beef or turkey

$3/4$ cup dried bread crumbs

(Ingredients continued on next page.)

You can get three different meals out of this one little recipe! You can serve your mini meat loaves the traditional way, with mashed potatoes and gravy, or you can call them "meatballs," put them in tomato sauce, and serve them with spaghetti. You can also place them on a bun for a savory burger. Any way you serve them, they're delicious!

I. Preheat the oven to 350°F.

2. In a food processor (with adult help), combine the onion, garlic, carrot, and Parmesan cheese. Process until finely chopped. ⚠

3. Pour the chopped mixture into a medium bowl. Add the meat, bread crumbs, tomato paste, Worcestershire sauce, oregano, egg, salt, and pepper and stir with a spoon until evenly mixed.

4. Spoon the meat mixture into the cups, filling them to the top.

5. Place the cups on a baking sheet and bake for 20 minutes, or until the juices in the cups are clear and the meat is brown all the way through. Cut one loaf down the middle to check. ⚠

6. Let cool for 5 minutes, then use a spoon to scoop the meat loaves out of the cups onto plates to serve. ⚠

Ingredients continued:

$1/4$ cup tomato paste or ketchup
2 tablespoons Worcestershire sauce
$1/8$ teaspoon dried oregano
1 egg
Pinch of salt
Pinch of pepper

Nacho Cups

Ingredients for 6 cups:

1 bag (16 ounces) tortilla chips
$3/4$ cup refried beans
$3/4$ cup chopped, cooked chicken (optional)
$1/8$ cup shredded Cheddar cheese
$1/8$ cup shredded Monterey Jack cheese
6 tablespoons salsa
6 tablespoons sour cream
$1/2$ avocado, peeled and cut into chunks

These tasty cups can be a meal or a snack, depending on how you serve them. With soup or salad, they make a great lunch or dinner. On their own, enjoy them as a snack or party food.

1. Preheat the oven to 350° F.

2. Place about five tortilla chips in each cup. Arrange them as shown in the photo on the left.

3. Put 2 tablespoons refried beans in each cup, on top of the chips. Then add 2 tablespoons chicken, if desired.

4. Sprinkle the cups evenly with the Cheddar and Jack cheeses.

5. Place the cups on a baking sheet and bake for about 10 minutes, or until the cheese is melted.

6. Top each cup with 1 tablespoon each salsa, sour cream, and avocado.

7. Serve in the cups, and pass extra chips for scooping out the dip!

> Nachos were named after Ignacio "Nacho" Anaya, the Mexican chef who invented the dish in 1943.

Fish with Salsa

Ingredients for 6 cups:

12 ounces fish fillet, no skin
(see suggestions on opposite page)
12 tablespoons favorite salsa
1/8 teaspoon garlic salt
1/4 cup olive oil

Salsa is more than a dip for chips. It's also a great cooking sauce. If you're not a big fan of fish, give it another chance with this recipe. See how good it tastes when topped with your favorite salsa!

I. Preheat the oven to 350°F.

2. Cut the fish fillet into 12 pieces. Each piece should be about 2 inches square. ⚠

3. Place 1 piece of fish in each cup.

4. Spoon 1 tablespoon salsa on top of the fish.

5. Top the salsa with another piece of fish, then add another tablespoon of salsa on top.

6. Sprinkle a little garlic salt into each cup. Then drizzle 2 teaspoons olive oil on top of each cup.

7. Place the cups on a baking sheet and bake for 20 minutes, or until the liquid on the top is bubbling. Serve in or out of the cups. ⚠

Fish and Salsa Ideas

Try halibut with a sweet salsa (like mango salsa), salmon with a tomato salsa, or any mild fish—tilapia, petrale sole, red snapper—with any salsa you like! And the fresher the fish, the better.

Quiche **with** Ham **and** Veggies

Ingredients for 6 quiches:

1 cup chopped asparagus or broccoli
3 eggs
Pinch of salt
Pinch of pepper
2 tablespoons milk
2 tablespoons grated Parmesan cheese
2 tablespoons shredded mozzarella cheese
Flour for work surface
$1/2$ pound puff pastry, thawed according
  to package directions if frozen
$1/4$ cup chopped ham

Quiches are yummy and packed with protein. You can enjoy these little savory pies in the morning for breakfast, with a salad for lunch, or as an appetizer before dinner. And if you don't like ham and veggies in your quiche, just pick other ingredients you like better!

1. Preheat the oven to 350°F.

2. Place the vegetable pieces in a microwave-safe bowl, and then add water to cover the vegetables. Microwave on high for 1 minute. Have an adult help remove the bowl from the microwave, drain the water, and set the vegetables aside. ⚠

3. Crack the eggs into a large measuring cup. Add the salt and pepper and stir with a fork until blended.

4. Add the milk and cheeses to the eggs and stir to mix.

5. To prepare the crust, sprinkle flour on a work surface. Then unfold the puff pastry so it lies flat.

6. Place a cup upside down on the dough and use a butter knife to cut around it. Repeat to make 6 disks total.

7. Place a pastry disk inside each cup. Press down to mold the disk to the bottom of the cup.

8. Arrange the cups on a baking sheet.

9. Fill each cup halfway with ham and vegetable pieces.

10. Pour the egg mixture into the cups, filling them to the top.

11. Bake the quiches for 20 minutes, or until there's no liquid in the center. Cool the quiches for 10 minutes, and then use a spoon to scoop them out of the cups. ⚠

Try it this way!

Quiches can be made with any type of meat and vegetables you like. Instead of the ham and veggies in this recipe, try 1/4 cup each chopped spinach and chopped, cooked chicken sausage. It's a delicious combination!

Chicken **Potpies**

Ingredients for 6 pies:

1 small carrot
1/4 yellow onion
3/4 cups cooked chicken, chopped
  in pea-size pieces
1/4 cup frozen peas, thawed
1 tablespoon all-purpose flour
Pinch of thyme
1/2 cup chicken stock
Pinch of garlic salt

(Ingredients continued on next page.)

If you love chicken potpie, try making your own miniature versions! With ready-made pastry dough and cooked chicken, these pies are easy and fun to prepare.

1. Preheat the oven to 350° F.

2. With adult help, cut the carrot and onion into pea-size pieces and put them in a medium bowl.

3. Add the chopped chicken, peas, flour, thyme, stock, garlic salt, and butter to the vegetable mixture and stir.

4. To prepare the crust, sprinkle flour on a work surface. Then unfold the puff pastry so it lies flat.

5. Place a cup upside down on the dough and use a butter knife to cut around it. Repeat to make 12 disks total. These will be your top and bottom crusts.

6. Place 1 disk in the bottom of each cup. Press down to mold the disk to the shape of the cup.

7. Spoon 2 tablespoons of the chicken mixture into each cup, on top of the pastry.

8. Place another pastry disk on the top of the chicken mixture to make each pie. You don't need to press the top and bottom crusts together. The top crust will just float on the filling, which will allow steam to escape as the pie cooks.

9. Put the pies in the freezer to chill for 10 minutes. This helps firm up the dough, so it will keep its shape better when you bake it.

Directions continued on next page.

Directions continued on next page.

Ingredients continued:

1 tablespoon butter
Flour for work surface
$1/2$ pound puff pastry, thawed according
to package directions if frozen

Try it this way!

- Try using turkey instead of chicken. Leftover roast turkey works great!

- Instead of cooking all of your pies right away, you can freeze some. Then you can pop them in the oven whenever you need a quick snack. Cook them at the same temperature and for the same amount of time as the unfrozen pies.

10. Place the cups on a baking sheet and bake for 20 minutes, or until you see bubbles on the edges of the pies. ⚠

11. Cool the pies for 10 minutes, then use a spoon to scoop the pies out onto plates. Serve warm!

Super Little Sides

Scalloped Potatoes

Ingredients for 6 cups:

6 small red potatoes
1 cup milk or heavy (whipping) cream
1 clove garlic, chopped
Pinch of salt
Pinch of pepper
1/2 cup shredded Swiss cheese

If you're not a big fan of scalloped potatoes, don't give up on them till you've tried this recipe. Red potatoes add great color and flavor to the dish. See what you think!

1. Preheat the oven to 350°F.

2. With adult help, cut each potato into rounds.

3. Stack the potato slices in each cup, one sliced potato per cup.

4. Pour the milk into a measuring cup, add the garlic, salt, and pepper and stir to mix.

5. Pour the milk mixture into the cups, to cover the potatoes.

6. Place the cups on a baking sheet and bake for 20 minutes, or until the liquid is bubbling. ⚠

7. Carefully sprinkle an equal amount of the cheese on top of each cup.

8. Bake for 2 more minutes, or until the cheese is golden brown. ⚠

You can use a ↗ cheese grater to cut the potatoes.

Roasted Summer Squash

Ingredients for 6 cups:

2 cups chopped summer squash,
   preferably pattypan
Pinch of salt
Pinch of pepper
1½ cups shredded Monterey
   Jack cheese

Summer squashes are harvested when they are young and tender (unlike winter squashes such as pumpkins, which are harvested when their skins are mature and thick). Try these little pattypan squashes roasted with cheese—they're delicious!

Pattypan squash

1. Preheat the oven to 350°F.

2. Put the squash pieces in a bowl, sprinkle with the salt and pepper, and stir to mix.

3. Fill the cups with the squash pieces and sprinkle the cheese on top.

4. Place the cups on a baking sheet and bake for 20 minutes, or until the liquid in the cup is bubbling. ⚠

Roasted Broccoli

Ingredients for 6 cups:

1 head broccoli
1 clove garlic, finely chopped
2 tablespoons olive oil
Pinch of salt
Pinch of pepper

Packed with all the good stuff—vitamin C, vitamin A, calcium, iron—broccoli is one of the best vegetables to eat. Now you can eat it packed with flavor!

1. Preheat the oven to 350°F.

2. With adult help, cut off and discard the broccoli stalk. Then chop or break apart the broccoli florets. ⚠

3. Combine the broccoli, garlic, olive oil, salt, and pepper in a medium bowl. Stir to mix.

4. Fill the cups with the broccoli mixture.

5. Place the cups on a baking sheet and roast for 20 minutes, or until the broccoli is tender. ⚠

Butternut Squash with Brown Sugar

Ingredients for 6 cups:

2 cups chopped butternut squash
(in bite-size cubes)
3 tablespoons butter
6 tablespoons light brown sugar,
lightly packed
6 tablespoons pine nuts (optional)

Butternut squash sure is tasty when it's roasted with butter and brown sugar! The pine nuts are optional, but they're good because they add a nice crunch and a nutty flavor.

1. Preheat the oven to 350°F.

2. Fill the cups with the squash cubes.

3. Put ½ tablespoon of butter on top of each cup.

4. Sprinkle each cup with 1 tablespoon brown sugar.

5. Place the cups on a baking sheet and bake for 40 minutes, or until the squash is tender when poked with a fork.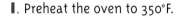

6. If you're using the pine nuts, have an adult help spread them on the baking sheet alongside the cups during the last 5 minutes of cooking.

7. Sprinkle the pine nuts on top of the cups right before serving.

Butternut squash is very good for you. It gives you plenty of vitamins A and C, and it's a good source of vitamin E, too!

Cauliflower Curry

Ingredients for 6 cups:

1 head cauliflower
$1/4$ teaspoon curry powder
Pinch of salt
Pinch of pepper
3 tablespoons butter

Cauliflower is often passed up in grocery stores—maybe because people like more colorful vegetables. But cauliflower definitely deserves attention. In this recipe, curry powder gives it a great sweet flavor!

1. Preheat the oven to 350°F.

2. With adult help, cut off and discard the cauliflower stem. Chop or break apart the cauliflower florets.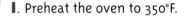

3. Combine the cauliflower, curry powder, salt, and pepper in a medium bowl. Stir to coat the cauliflower with the seasonings.

4. Fill the cups with the cauliflower mixture. Then put a small pat ($1/2$ tablespoon) of butter on top of each cup.

5. Place the cups on a baking sheet and roast for 20 minutes, or until the cauliflower is tender when poked with a fork.

Candied Carrots

Candied carrots are a great side dish with roasted meats, especially chicken or pork. For a beef dinner, you can leave out the brown sugar for a more savory taste.

Ingredients for 6 cups:

6 carrots, sliced into rounds
$^{1}/_{4}$ cup light brown sugar, lightly packed
$^{1}/_{4}$ teaspoon dried thyme
2 tablespoons water
3 tablespoons butter, softened

1. Preheat the oven to 350°F.

2. Combine the carrots, brown sugar, and thyme in a medium bowl. Mix together with your hands.

3. Fill the cups with the carrots. Add 1 teaspoon water to each cup.

4. Top each cup with a small pat ($^{1}/_{2}$ tablespoon) of butter.

5. Place the cups on a baking sheet and bake for 20 minutes, or until the carrots are tender when poked with a fork. ⚠

Crispy Potato Nests

Ingredients for 6 cups:

1 large russet potato
2 tablespoons olive oil
1 teaspoon garlic salt

Crispy potato nests are just plain fun to make. They're beautiful on a plate by themselves, or you can fill them with a green salad. They taste a lot like French fries, and they make a plate of food a piece of art!

1. Preheat the oven to 425°F.

2. Scrub the potato with a sponge or vegetable brush.

3. With adult help, grate the potato into long thin strips. ⚠

4. Put the grated potato in a medium bowl and add the olive oil and garlic salt. Mix well.

5. Turn the cups upside down onto a baking sheet. Wrap 3 to 4 tablespoons of the potato mixture onto the bottom and down the sides of each cup, forming an upside-down nest. Repeat with the remaining potato mixture to make 6 nests total.

6. Bake for 15 to 20 minutes, or until the nests are browned and crisp. ⚠

7. With adult help, use a spatula to remove the cups from the baking sheet to a work surface. Let them cool for 10 minutes. ⚠

8. Carefully slide out each cup. Now you have 6 nests you can fill with anything you want. Check out the list below for some ideas!

Great Nest Fillers

· Fill the nests with a salad of mixed greens, cooked chicken or turkey (chopped into bite-size pieces), and your favorite salad dressing.

· Put the nests in small bowls and spoon chili on top. Then serve with toppings like shredded cheese, sour cream, and olives.

· Serve your nests with applesauce inside and a dollop of sour cream on top, like potato pancakes!

Corn and Zucchini Mélange

Ingredients for 6 cups:

2 ears sweet white corn, or 1 cup
    frozen corn kernels
2 small zucchini, chopped into
    bite-size pieces
1/2 red onion, chopped into
    bite-size pieces
1/2 cup shredded mozzarella cheese
2 tablespoons grated Parmesan cheese
Pinch of salt
Pinch of pepper

Mélange is a French word for "mixture," and this tasty mixture of corn, zucchini, and cheese is sure to please! Fresh corn will give you the best taste and texture, but you can use frozen kernels when fresh corn is out of season.

1. Preheat the oven to 350°F.

2. If you're using fresh corn, shuck the ears of corn. Then ask an adult to cut the kernels off the cobs. ⚠

3. Combine the corn kernels, zucchini, onion, mozzarella cheese, Parmesan cheese, salt, and pepper in a medium bowl. Stir to mix well.

4. Fill the cups with the corn mixture.

5. Place the cups on a baking sheet and bake for about 30 minutes, or until the zucchini is tender when poked with a fork. ⚠

Baked Polenta Cups

Ingredients for 6 cups:

3 tablespoons butter
1¼ cups yellow cornmeal
1½ cups chicken stock
⅛ cup grated Parmesan cheese
Extra Parmesan cheese for
sprinkling (optional)

Polenta is a traditional northern Italian dish made from cornmeal. You can serve it as a side dish with butter, or you can top it with tomato sauce. It's great with Parmesan cheese sprinkled on top, too, as you'll see when you try this recipe!

1. Preheat the oven to 350°F.

2. Place a slice of butter in the bottom of each cup.

3. Add 2 tablespoons cornmeal to each cup.

4. Add ¼ cup chicken stock to each cup.

5. Sprinkle a teaspoon of Parmesan on top of each cup.

6. Place the cups on a baking sheet and bake for 20 minutes, or until all liquid is gone. ⚠️

7. Let the cups cool for 5 minutes, then turn them upside down onto plates for a beautiful presentation. Sprinkle a little more Parmesan on top if you want!

Great Polenta Toppers

• Top your polenta with your favorite vegetables, steamed in the microwave (following the steaming directions on page 26). Add a dollop of butter on top, and you have a great side dish.

• Instead of topping the polenta with just tomato sauce, mix vegetables (like zucchini or bell peppers) into the sauce. Have an adult help cook the vegetables in the sauce until they're tender.

Herb and Cheese Risotto

Ingredients for 6 cups:

1½ cups Arborio rice
¼ cup grated Parmesan cheese
½ teaspoon dried thyme
Pinch of salt
Pinch of pepper
3 cups chicken stock

Risotto is an Italian rice dish made with special rice varieties, like Arborio. These kinds of rice have wider, more rounded grains than the long-grain rice you're probably used to. Risotto can be prepared with lots of different ingredients. Try this recipe with cheese and herbs. It is a wonderful side dish with any meat or fish!

1. Preheat the oven to 350°F.

2. Combine the rice, cheese, thyme, salt, and pepper in a medium bowl. Stir to mix well.

3. Put 2 tablespoons of the rice mixture in each cup.

4. Place the cups on a baking sheet. Pour the stock into the cups, filling them to the top.

5. Bake for 20 minutes, or until all the liquid has been absorbed and the rice is tender. ⚠️

6. Let the cups cool for 5 minutes, then turn the risotto out onto plates to serve. *Perfecto!*

Arborio rice →

Baked Rice Cups

Ingredients for each cup:

2 tablespoons rice
$\frac{1}{4}$ cup water

Optional Ingredients:

- To add some flavor to your rice, try a pinch of thyme or sweet curry powder.
- For more flavor, use chicken broth instead of water.
- To add color, try a pinch of saffron.

Here's an easy way to make rice—and the little rice cups look fantastic when you turn them out onto a plate!

1. Preheat the oven to 350°F.

2. Measure the rice into each cup.

3. Place the cups on a baking sheet. Then pour the water into each cup.

4. Bake for 20 minutes, or until all the liquid is absorbed and the rice is tender. ⚠

5. Let cool for 5 minutes, then turn the rice out onto plates for a beautiful presentation!

Sweet Treats

Classic **Cupcakes**

Ingredients for 18 cupcakes:

2 cups all-purpose flour
2 teaspoons baking powder
1/4 teaspoon salt
1/2 cup (1 stick) plus 2 tablespoons butter, softened
1 1/4 cups sugar
4 eggs
1 teaspoon vanilla extract
3/4 cup milk

Who doesn't love cupcakes? And what better way to bake them than in silicone cups! This is a light yellow cake recipe that'll be delicious with any icing you choose.

1. Preheat the oven to 350°F.

2. Combine the flour, baking powder, and salt in a medium bowl and stir to mix. Set aside.

3. Combine the butter and sugar in a large bowl. With adult help, beat with an electric mixer on high speed until you have light crumbs of butter and sugar. ⚠

4. Add the eggs and vanilla to the butter mixture and continue to beat until everything is well combined.

5. Slowly add the flour mixture to the egg mixture and mix thoroughly.

6. Add the milk and mix until blended.

7. Spoon the batter into the cups, filling them two-thirds full.

8. Place the cups on a baking sheet and bake for 15 to 20 minutes, or until a butter knife or toothpick inserted into a cupcake comes out clean.

9. Let the cupcakes cool for 20 minutes. Then gently peel back the cups to release the cupcakes so you can bake your next batch. (No need to wash the cups between batches!)

Brownies

Ingredients for 12 brownies:

2 large squares (1 ounce each)
   unsweetened chocolate, chopped
1/2 cup (1 stick) butter
2 eggs
1 cup sugar
1 teaspoon vanilla extract
1/2 cup all-purpose flour
1/8 teaspoon salt
1/2 cup semisweet chocolate chips

There's nothing better than a batch of homemade brownies that are full of fresh ingredients and contain nothing artificial (like you often find in a boxed mix). They melt in your mouth with rich chocolate flavor!

1. Preheat the oven to 350°F.

2. Put the chocolate and the butter in a microwave-safe bowl. With adult help, microwave on high for 15 seconds. Then stir the chocolate. If the mixture isn't smooth, return to the microwave for another 15 seconds, and repeat until melted.

3. In another bowl, using a fork, beat the eggs until thick. Add the sugar and mix well.

4. Add the chocolate mixture and mix thoroughly.

5. Add the vanilla, flour, and salt and stir until combined.

6. Stir in the chocolate chips.

7. Place the cups on a baking sheet. Pour half of the batter into the cups, filling them to the top.

8. Bake for 30 minutes, or until the tops crack. Then insert a butter knife or a toothpick into a brownie to see if the center is done. Cool for 15 minutes, and then gently peel back the cups. If the brownies don't come out easily, cool for 5 more minutes. ⚠

9. Refill the cups to make 6 more brownies the same way.

Little **Pear** Pies

Ingredients for 6 pies:

Serve these sweet little pies topped with vanilla ice cream or whipped cream!

Pear Pies
Flour for work surface
$^1/_2$ pound puff pastry, thawed according
   to package directions if frozen
3 ripe pears
$^1/_4$ cup light brown sugar, lightly packed
$^1/_8$ teaspoon ground cinnamon
2 tablespoons all-purpose flour

(Ingredients continued on next page.)

To Make the Pear Pies

1. Sprinkle your work surface with flour, and then unfold the puff pastry so it lies flat.

2. Place a cup upside down on the dough and use a butter knife to cut around it. Repeat to make 6 disks total.

3. Place a disk in the bottom of each cup. Press down to mold the disk to the shape of the cup.

4. Put the cups in the freezer for 10 minutes. This helps firm up the dough, so it keeps its shape better when you bake it.

5. While the cups are chilling, peel and core the pears and then chop into small pieces. ⚠️

6. Combine the pears, brown sugar, cinnamon, and flour in a medium bowl and stir to mix.

7. Remove the cups from the freezer, and fill the cups with the pear mixture.

To Make the Crumb Topping and Bake the Pies

1. Preheat the oven to 350°F.

2. Combine the brown sugar, granulated sugar, flour, cinnamon, and butter in a bowl. Mix the ingredients with a fork until you have pea-size crumbs.

3. Sprinkle an equal amount of the topping on each pie, covering the pears.

4. Place the cups on a baking sheet and bake for 30 minutes, or until the tops of the pies are nicely browned. Cool for 10 minutes, then gently turn out of the cups. ⚠

Ingredients continued:

Crumb Topping
¹/₂ cup light brown sugar, lightly packed
¹/₂ cup granulated sugar
6 tablespoons all-purpose flour
1 tablespoon ground cinnamon
¹/₂ cup (1 stick) butter, softened

Tiny **Fruit** Tarts

Ingredients for 6 tarts:

Crust
9 graham crackers
1/3 cup granulated sugar
1/2 cup (1 stick) butter,
  melted and cooled

(Ingredients continued on next page.)

If you like graham crackers, you'll love these little fruit tarts with their buttery graham-cracker crusts. Fill them with your favorite fruit, like whole blueberries, sliced strawberries, peach cubes, or banana slices. Any fruit goes with whipped cream and graham crackers!

To Make the Crust

1. Preheat the oven to 350°F.

2. Put the graham crackers and the granulated sugar in a zippered plastic bag, press out the air, and seal closed. Using a mallet or rolling pin, crush the crackers. The cracker crumbs will mix with the sugar as you crush. Keep crushing until the mixture looks like sand.

3. Pour the graham cracker mixture into a medium bowl. Add the melted butter and mix together with a fork.

4. Place 2 tablespoons of the crust mixture into each cup and press down with the back of a spoon.

5. Place the cups on a baking sheet and bake for 7 minutes, or until browned. Let the cups cool completely before filling.

To Make the Filling and Fill the Tarts

1. Pour the cream into a medium bowl. Using an electric mixer (with adult help), beat on high speed until soft peaks form.

2. Add the cream cheese, vanilla, and powdered sugar and continue to beat on high speed until stiff peaks form.

3. Spoon the whipped cream filling into the cooled crusts. Then top with the fruit of your choice.

4. Serve the tarts in or out of the cups. To serve out of the cups, use a spoon to gently scoop out the tarts.

Ingredients continued:

Filling
1 cup heavy (whipping) cream
3 tablespoons cream cheese, softened
1/8 teaspoon vanilla extract
1/4 cup powdered sugar
Fresh fruit

Lemon **Bars**

Ingredients for 12 bars:

Crust
½ cup (1 stick) butter
¼ cup powdered sugar
1 cup all-purpose flour
2 tablespoons heavy (whipping) cream

(Ingredients continued on next page.)

Here's an idea: Instead of selling lemonade, open a lemon bar stand! These bright yellow bars are a refreshing treat that will attract lots of customers!

To Make the Crust

1. Using a food processor (with adult help), combine the butter, powdered sugar, and flour and process until large crumbs form.

2. Add the cream and process just until the dough comes together in a rough ball. ⚠️

3. Place two tablespoons of the dough into a cup. Press the dough evenly to form a crust on the bottom of the cup. Do this six times until each cup has a crust.

4. Place the cups in the freezer to chill for 10 minutes. This helps firm up the dough, so it will keep its shape better when you bake it.

To Make the Filling and Bake the Bars

1. Preheat the oven to 350°F.

2. Combine the eggs and sugar in a medium bowl. Using an electric mixer (with adult help), beat on high speed until the mixture is pale yellow. ⚠️

3. Add the lemon zest and lemon juice to the egg mixture and beat on high speed until combined. ⚠️

4. Add the flour and baking powder and beat on high speed again until well mixed. ⚠️

5. Place the chilled cups on a baking sheet. Pour the lemon mixture into the cups, filling them two-thirds full.

6. Bake for 20 minutes, or until the filling doesn't jiggle when you shake the baking sheet. ⚠️

7. Cool the bars for 20 minutes. Then use a spoon to gently scoop the bars from the cups so you can make your next batch.

8. Store your lemon bars in the refrigerator until you're ready to eat them, but serve them at room temperature.

Ingredients continued:

Lemon Filling
2 large eggs
1 cup granulated sugar
1 tablespoon grated lemon zest
$^1/_3$ cup fresh lemon juice
2 tablespoons all-purpose flour
$^1/_2$ teaspoon baking powder

Mini **Strawberry** Shortcakes

Ingredients for 12 cakes:

18 Classic Cupcakes (pages 50–51)
2 pints strawberries
1 cup heavy (whipping) cream
3 tablespoons powdered sugar

Packed with vitamin C, strawberries are really good for you. Add them to these delicious cupcakes, and you have a dessert with little added sugar that will satisfy any sweet tooth.

1. Make the Classic Cupcakes (on pages 50–51) and let them cool completely.

2. Cut off the stems of the strawberries. Cut the berries lengthwise into quarters. ⚠

3. Combine the cream and powdered sugar in a large bowl. Using an electric mixer (with adult help), beat on high speed until soft peaks form. ⚠

4. Cut each cupcake in half horizontally, and place the bottom half on a plate. Put a big spoonful of whipped cream on the cupcake bottom, then top with strawberries.

5. Top each strawberry shortcake with a cupcake top. Then add one more dollop of whipped cream and a few more sliced strawberries for garnish.

Ice-Cream Sandwiches

Ingredients for 6 sandwiches:

1 pint ice cream
(any flavor you like)
12 Oreo cookies
5 tablespoons butter, melted

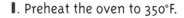
These are not your ordinary ice-cream sandwiches! The chocolate cookie crust delivers a big crunch and goes with any ice cream—just pick your favorite flavor!

1. Preheat the oven to 350°F.

2. Take the ice cream out of the freezer and let thaw until melted.

3. Put the cookies in a zippered plastic bag, force out the air, and seal closed. Then crush the cookies with a rolling pin or mallet until the crumbs are like sand. (Or, ask an adult to crush the cookies in a food processor.) ⚠️

4. Combine the cookie crumbs and melted butter in a medium bowl and stir until well mixed.

5. Put 1 tablespoon of the crumb mixture in each cup. Press it down with your fingers to form an even disk in the bottom of the cup.

6. Place the cups on a baking sheet and bake for 5 minutes, or until the cookies look firm and dry.

7. Cool the cookies completely, for at least 20 minutes.

8. Pour the melted ice cream into 3 of the cups, filling them all the way.

9. Turn the cookies out of the other 3 cups. Put 1 cookie on top of each ice cream–filled cup.

10. Freeze the sandwiches for about 1 hour.

11. Remove the sandwiches from the cups, following the instructions on the right.

12. Serve the sandwiches immediately, or wrap in waxed paper and place in the freezer until serving.

13. When the first 3 sandwiches are made, repeat steps 5 to 12 to make 3 more delicious sandwiches!

To remove the sandwiches:

- Fill a small bowl about half full with warm water.

- Place each cup in the water, immersing halfway, for 5 seconds.

- Remove the cup, turn it over, and squeeze the bottom. If the sandwich doesn't slip out, return the cup to the water for another 5 seconds.

Compliments to the Chef!

It's very satisfying to make something and then to hear people say, "This tastes good!" So, what was your most successful dish? Which recipe would you make again? And again?

Once you're comfortable with a recipe, see if you can find ways to make it your own, with different or extra ingredients. All great chefs experiment like that, and you can, too. That's the fun part!

So, enjoy your silicone cups, and let the compliments to the chef roll in!

About the Author

Julia Myall has worked as a chef in many premier San Francisco restaurants and as a cooking teacher at the American Embassy in Paris. She is now the mother of three wonderful and tremendously active children. She lives in Lafayette, California.